EYE TO EYE WITH DOGS

ROTTWEILERS

Lynn M. Stone

Publishing LLC
Vero Beach, Florida 32964

www.rourkepublishing.com

Title page: *The Rottweiler is a popular family dog.*

Acknowledgments: For their help in the preparation of this book, the author thanks Mechelle and Trent Clark, Kathy Fluery, Pam Grant, and Carol Krickeberg.

Photo Credits: All photos © Lynn M. Stone

Editor: Frank Sloan

Cover and page design by Nicola Stratford

Library of Congress Cataloging-in-Publication Data

Stone, Lynn M.
  Rottweilers / Lynn M. Stone.
      p. cm. -- (Eye to eye with dogs II)
  Includes bibliographical references and index.
  ISBN 1-59515-161-3 (hardcover)
  1. Rottweiler dog--Juvenile literature. I. Title. II. Series: Stone, Lynn M. Eye to eye with dogs II.
  SF429.R7S757 2004
  636.73--dc22

                                                    2004008026

Printed in the USA

CG/CG

Table of Contents

The Rottweiler, named for a town in Germany, is one of the most common dogs in North America.

The Rottweiler

One hundred years ago, the Rottweiler had nearly disappeared. Today the big, powerful Rottweiler is one of the most common **breeds** in North America.

ROTTWEILER FACTS

Weight: 80-135 pounds
(36-61 kilograms)

Height: 22-27 inches
(56-69 centimeters)

Country of Origin:
Germany

Life Span: 8-11 years

Rottweilers were popular in Germany, especially near the town of Rottweil, for hundreds of years. They were known as the "butcher dogs of Rottweil." They herded cattle to butcher shops for slaughter. They also hauled carts.

Rottweiler pups became rare when the cattle business in southern Germany changed.

The Rottweiler's large, powerful body and jaws once made it a popular police and military dog.

A Rottweiler shows balance in an agility test.

In the mid-1850s, cattle driving was forbidden, and donkey carts and trains replaced dog carts. The public had little use for its "butcher dogs," *Metzgerhunds*.

In the early 1900s, dog lovers formed clubs to save the Rottweiler breed. One club encouraged the use of Rottweilers as police dogs.

The breed's popularity grew in the 1920s. People in North America took notice of Rottweilers. The American Kennel Club added the Rottweiler to its breed list in 1931. Its fame grew to the point that it was once the second most popular breed in the United States.

A Rottweiler should be treated with great respect, especially if it's a dog unknown to you.

A Rottweiler bounds over a hurdle in an agility test.

Rottweilers are popular as companions, watchdogs, and guard dogs. Because they learn easily and are athletic, they do well in both **obedience** and **agility** events.

This female (right) and male (left) enjoy each other's company.

The Dog for You?

Most Rottweilers have not been trained as guard dogs or to be **aggressive**.

They are generally quiet, loyal, and loving companions. But Rottweilers are protective of their owners. They can be fierce in defense of their human families, especially if they are trained to be.

Rottweilers are large, strong, calm, and quite sure of themselves. They are not shy, and they don't immediately warm to strangers. They generally don't like other dogs. Unlike some breeds, a Rottweiler seems content to be the only dog in a home.

After obedience training, a Rottweiler takes time out for a brushing.

Rottweilers enjoy life outdoors where they can sniff, romp, and retrieve tennis balls.

A Rottweiler can live outdoors, but it needs plenty of contact time with its owners. It also needs daily exercise time and obedience training. The Rottweiler is a powerful animal. It needs to be under its owner's control.

Rottweilers do not do well in extremely hot or cold temperatures. They prefer cool days to warm.

The Rottweiler has straight, medium length hair that requires little grooming.

Cool autumn weather is ideal for a Rottweiler.

The ancestors of modern Rottweilers probably didn't look much different than their modern cousins.

Rottweilers of the Past

Dogs similar to Rottweilers were probably used to drive and guard cattle by the **ancient** Romans. About 1,900 years ago, Roman soldiers with their cattle marched into southern Germany and what would become the town of Rottweil. The Roman armies lived on the cattle that their dogs drove.

As the Romans settled in Germany, their herd dogs settled with them. These dogs were likely the direct **ancestors** of today's Rottweilers.

Looks

The Rottweiler is a large black dog with light brown trim on its face, neck, chest, and legs. A Rottweiler has a short, **docked** tail, like a boxer.

The first Rottweiler pups were probably raised by the ancient Romans.

Rottweilers' tails are docked when they are small.

The Rottweiler has a deep chest and sturdy legs on a solid body. It has a broad head and a fairly short muzzle. It has hanging, medium sized ears and dark eyes.

Like its ancestors, modern Rottweilers look similar to mastiffs and bullmastiffs. Mastiffs and bullmastiffs, however, have more bulldog-like faces than do Rottweilers. The mastiff is a much larger dog, too. It weighs up to 190 pounds (86 kg).

Rottweilers are sturdy dogs with broad skulls and hanging ears.

Always alert, a Rottweiler patrols its family's goldfish pond.

Because they are fairly easy to train, some Rottweilers become search-and-rescue dogs. Many of them worked hard in New York City after the September 11, 2001 attacks on the World Trade Center.

A Note about Dogs

Puppies are cute and cuddly, but only after serious thought should anybody buy one. Puppies grow up.

And remember that a dog will require more than love and patience. It will need healthy food, exercise, grooming, a warm, safe place in which to live, and medical care.

A dog can be your best friend, but you need to be its best friend, too.

Choosing the right breed requires some homework. For more information about buying and owning a dog, contact the American Kennel Club at http://www.akc.org/index.cfm or the Canadian Kennel Club at http://www.ckc.ca/.

Glossary

aggressive (uh GRES iv) — wanting to attacking or attacking

agility (uh JIL uh tee) — the ability to perform certain athletic tasks, such as leaping through a hoop

ancestor (AN SES tur) — an animal that at some past time was part of the modern animal's family

ancient (AIN shunt) — of a time long ago

breeds (BREEDZ) — particular kinds of domestic animals within a larger, closely related group, such as the Rottweiler breed within the dog group

docked (DOCKD) — to have been cut, or clipped off

obedience (o BEED ee unts) — the willingness to follow someone's direction or command; a pre-set training program for dogs

Index

Further Reading

Beauchamp, Richard. *Rottweilers for Dummies.* John Wiley & Sons, 2000
Carroll, David L. *The ASPCA Complete Guide to Pet Care.* Plume, 2001
Fogle, Bruce. *The Dog Owner's Manual.* DK Publishing, 2003
Wilcox, Charlotte. *Rottweiler.* Capstone, 2000

Websites to Visit

American Rottweiler Club at www.amrottclub.org

About the Author

Lynn M. Stone is the author of more than 400 children's books. He is a talented natural history photographer as well. Lynn, a former teacher, travels worldwide to photograph wildlife in its natural habitat.